Bruno Solnik
HEC School of Management
Jouy en Josas
France

Predictable Time-Varying Components of International Asset Returns

The Research Foundation of
The Institute of Chartered Financial Analysts

Research Foundation Publications

Active Currency Management
by Murali Ramaswami

Canadian Stocks, Bonds, Bills, and Inflation: 1950–1987
by James E. Hatch and Robert E. White

Closed-Form Duration Measures and Strategy Applications
by Nelson J. Lacey and Sanjay K. Nawalkha

Corporate Bond Rating Drift: An Examination of Credit Quality Rating Changes Over Time
by Edward I. Altman and Duen Li Kao

Default Risk, Mortality Rates, and the Performance of Corporate Bonds
by Edward I. Altman

Durations of Nondefault-Free Securities
by Gerald O. Bierwag and George G. Kaufman

Earnings Forecasts and Share Price Reversals
by Werner F.M. De Bondt

The Effect of Illiquidity on Bond Price Data: Some Symptoms and Remedies
by Oded Sarig and Arthur Warga

Equity Trading Costs
by Hans R. Stoll

Ethics, Fairness, Efficiency, and Financial Markets
by Hersh Shefrin and Meir Statman

Ethics in the Investment Profession: A Survey
by E. Theodore Veit, CFA, and Michael R. Murphy, CFA

The Founders of Modern Finance: Their Prize-Winning Concepts and 1990 Nobel Lectures

Initial Public Offerings: The Role of Venture Capitalists
by Joseph T. Lim and Anthony Saunders

A New Method for Valuing Treasury Bond Futures Options
by Ehud I. Ronn and Robert R. Bliss, Jr.

A New Perspective on Asset Allocation
by Martin L. Leibowitz

Options and Futures: A Tutorial
by Roger G. Clarke

The Poison Pill Anti-Takeover Defense: The Price of Strategic Deterrence
by Robert F. Bruner

Program Trading and Systematic Risk
by A.J. Senchack, Jr., and John D. Martin

The Role of Risk Tolerance in the Asset Allocation Process: A New Perspective
by W.V. Harlow III, CFA, and Keith C. Brown, CFA

Selecting Superior Securities
by Marc R. Reinganum

Stock Market Structure, Volatility, and Volume
by Hans R. Stoll and Robert E. Whaley

Stocks, Bonds, Bills, and Inflation: Historical Returns (1926–1987)
by Roger G. Ibbotson and Rex A. Sinquefield
(Published with Business One Irwin)

Predictable Time-Varying Components of International Asset Returns

ISBN 0-943205-20-4

Printed in the United States of America

August 1993

Mission

The mission of the Research Foundation is to identify, fund, and publish research material that:
- expands the body of relevant and useful knowledge available to practitioners;
- assists practitioners in understanding and applying this knowledge; and
- enhances the investment management community's effectiveness in serving clients.

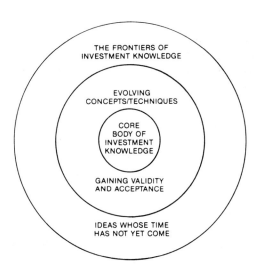

The Research Foundation of
The Institute of Chartered Financial Analysts
P.O. Box 3668
Charlottesville, Virginia 22903
U.S.A.
Telephone: 804/977-6600
Fax: 804/977-1103

Foreword

The importance of investing in international assets cannot be overemphasized. Partly because international investing is still in its infancy, however, research on the relative merits of this investment alternative remains sparse. The risk and return patterns observed for various asset classes across different countries is of particular interest to investments practitioners.

Solnik advances our understanding of how international asset returns and risks vary over time. In this vein, the author provides risk–return benchmarks that are useful in implementing international investment programs. Of particular importance are Solnik's findings about the predictability of the time-varying component of expected returns, even though the length of the reversion time varies across asset classes.

The author posits that practitioners often look for trends in the short run (positive autocorrelation of short-term returns) and reversion to fundamental values over the long run (negative autocorrelation of long-term returns). It is with respect to the time patterns of long-term returns that this research is especially valuable. Among three major asset classes (stocks, bonds, and currencies) in eight different countries, Solnik finds that returns follow a mean-reversion process. Thus, expected returns can be predicted based on past realized returns.

Solnik proposes that technical analysis could be used to detect meaningful trends and reversions, but he cautions that changes in the length of time of mean reversion could render these technical models useless.

Solnik's findings may appear to be inconsistent with markets in equilibrium. After closer inspection, the results are more consistent with the presence of business cycles among markets in equilibrium.

The Research Foundation is pleased to sponsor Solnik's work on international risk and return. He has contributed to the understanding of a vital topic that will be at the forefront of investments thought and inquiry for a long time to come.

John W. Peavy III, CFA

Predictable Time-Varying Components of International Asset Returns

International investment management has been growing rapidly during the past 10 years in all developed countries. International assets of U.S. tax-exempt institutions, for example, have grown at a rate of more than 25 percent a year since 1988. The bulk of cross-border assets are in international equities, but international fixed-income investments are also growing rapidly.

Investment managers have come to realize that, in a global context, the asset-allocation decision is the major explanation of differences in portfolio performance. The selection of individual securities has much less impact on the performance of a diversified global portfolio. Therefore, the focus of international financial analysis is moving from the study of individual companies to the study of national markets and currencies.

In parallel, recent academic research suggests that measures of expected returns and risk have a predictable time-varying component. Such time variation is not inconsistent with the well-accepted theories of market equilibrium, which never claimed that measures of risk or expected returns should be constant over time. Clearly, predictable time variation is of great practical relevance to investment managers.

The purpose of this paper is to review the major approaches to modeling the time variation in asset returns and to illustrate their applications in a global context. The discussion will not be exhaustive or contain the latest theoretical sophistication, but it will describe those methods that can be of most practical use to financial analysts and investment managers.

Mathematical developments are kept to a minimum, and readers should consult referenced articles for detailed derivations. A minimal set of notations and concepts do need to be defined, however. The basic idea is that the expected return on an asset over period $t + 1$, $E\ (R_{t+1}|\ \Phi_t)$, and its variance, $\mathrm{VAR}(R_{t+1}|\ \Phi_t)$, can be predicted at time t based on a public information set, Φ_t, that is observable at the start of the period. The models are functions of the information set considered. *Conditional* is the term for the distribution of asset returns in which the expected return and variance (the *moments*) are allowed to vary over time on the basis of (conditional on) observable information set Φ_t. *Unconditional* is the term for the distribution of asset returns in which the expected return and variance are assumed constant over time. This definition is equivalent to assuming that information set Φ_t reduces to a constant. The unconditional mean and variance are typically estimated from historical data by taking the sample mean and variance.

The various approaches to modeling time variation in expected returns will be illustrated with stock and bond data from France, Germany, the Netherlands, Switzerland, the United Kingdom, Japan, Canada, and the United States—capital markets for which the data are of good quality. Together, these markets account for 90 percent of world market capitalization.

The data on international financial markets vary greatly in availability, quality, and comparability. The quality of data is important, however, if one is to avoid spurious forecasting ability based on poor data measurement. The study covers the period from January 1960 to December 1991 for equity and cash investments, for which period month-end data are available for eight national stock indexes and exchange rates. Prior to 1970, however, active and free markets for long-term and short-term fixed-income instruments did not exist in the countries used in this study except in the United States and the United Kingdom.[1] Interest rates were set at artificial levels by the governments of most other countries. Therefore, to ensure high-quality data, especially for bonds and short-term interest rates, the study uses bond indexes only for the 1971–91 period. Because of the higher quality interest rate data since 1971, the general focus of the study is on this later period. The data are described in the appendix.

The next two sections of the study deal with models of expected returns, specifically with models of expected returns based on past realized returns, which is sometimes known as *mean reversion* in asset prices, and models in which time variation in expected returns is predicted on the basis of a set of fundamental variables. The subsequent section introduces models of the volatility of asset returns that incorporate past volatility and shocks. In the final sections, dynamic strategies are designed that use the conditional risk-premium models previously introduced. The models' performance is studied, and the issue of currency hedging is discussed.

---

[1] See for example, observations about Japan by Campbell and Hamao (1992).

Mean-Reversion Models

Practitioners tend to believe that past returns can be used to forecast future returns. They often look for trends in the short run (positive autocorrelation of short-term returns) and reversion to fundamental values over the long run (negative autocorrelation of long-term returns). The autocorrelation in returns comes from the autocorrelation in transitory expected returns. The rationale for expecting short-term positive autocorrelation is intuitive: Expectations depend on current economic conditions, and these economic conditions change slowly over time. In the long run, economic conditions and expected returns should revert to normal long-term trends. This pattern of positive short-term correlation and negative long-term correlation is consistent with business cycles.

Several econometric studies have demonstrated the presence of serial correlation in asset returns.[2] Positive autocorrelation is indeed generally found for short-term returns, and negative autocorrelation for long-term returns.

The stochastic return on an asset can be written as

$$R_{t+1} = E\ (R_{t+1}|\ \Phi_t) + \varepsilon_{t+1}\,, \tag{1}$$

where R_{t+1} is the asset return over period $t + 1$, $E(R_{t+1}|\Phi_t)$ is its conditional expected return based on the Φ_t information set observable at time t, and ε_{t+1} is a pure noise term with zero mean and no serial correlation. The conditional expected return is assumed to be made up of a permanent component, R^* (the unconditional mean return), and a transitory component, m_t (which is serially correlated with a mean of zero), in such a way that

$$E\ (R_{t+1}|\Phi_t) = R^* + m_t\,. \tag{2}$$

In computing the autocorrelation, one looks at deviations from the unconditional mean return, i.e., deviations from the sample mean return, R^*. The unconditional autocorrelation with a k-month lag, ρ_k, is as follows:

---

[2] See Cutler, Poterba, and Summers (1991); Cecchetti and Lam (1990); Conrad and Kaul (1989); Chan (1988); Fama and French (1988b); Kandel and Stambaugh (1988); Lo and McKinley (1988); Poterba and Summers (1988); and Keim and Stambaugh (1986). These articles discuss autocorrelograms and variance tests.

$$\rho_k = \mathrm{cor}(R_t, R_{t-k}) = E\left[(R_t - R^*)(R_{t-k} - R^*)\right]$$
$$= E\left[(m_t + \varepsilon_t)(m_{t-k} + \varepsilon_{t-k})\right] \tag{3}$$
$$= E\left(m_t, m_{t-k}\right).$$

Empirical Findings.   Table 1 reports the autocorrelation data for the eight major stock markets from January 1960 to December 1991. The first two columns give the sample (unconditional) mean return and standard deviation. The next four columns give the autocorrelation with lags of 1, 2, 3, and 12 months. The last three columns report the average autocorrelation over one year (lag of 1 to 12 months), two years (lag of 13 to 24 months), and three years (lag of 25 to 36 months). Calculations are performed in local currency in the top panel and in U.S. dollars in the bottom panel. The local-currency returns are the most pertinent for this analysis. Evidence of positive one-month autocorrelation for each national stock market is clear. Nontrading could explain part of this phenomenon, but the autocorrelation is too large to be explained solely by a technical factor. Evidence of mean reversion after two years is also clear: The two-year autocorrelations are negative for each market.

Table 2 reports similar statistics for currency returns over the 1960–91 period. These returns are equal to the U.S. dollar return in foreign short-term deposits. Most of the short-term correlations (from one to three months) are positive. The one-year autocorrelations are all positive. The three-year correlations tend to be negative.

Table 3 reports the statistics for bond returns for the 1971–91 period. For the sake of comparison, autocorrelations for stocks and currency returns are also reported for the 1971–91 period in Tables 4 and 5. Again, bond returns tend to be positively correlated over the short term (one year) and negatively correlated over the long term (two and three years). The results confirm the findings of Cutler, Poterba, and Summers (1991) for a different time period. The mean-reversion phenomenon reported for the U.S. market by Poterba and Summers (1988) and Lo and McKinley (1988) is also shown to be true for international markets.

Practical Implications.   The positive and negative autocorrelations are observed statistical phenomena, but they provide evidence to support the use of technical analysis and related techniques. The problem is to determine the proper technical model and data frequency to use, both of which depend on the market being considered. For example, the positive autocorrelation is a short-term phenomenon for stock markets, and the mean reversion seems to take place within two years. Positive autocorrelation seems to be longer lived (one or two years) for currencies, and mean reversion takes several years.

TABLE 1. Stock Markets: Sample Statistics, 1960–91

Country	Mean Return (per month)	Standard Deviation (per month)	Autocorrelation				Yearly Averages		
			1-Month Lag	2-Month Lag	3-Month Lag	12-Month Lag	1 Year (lag 1 to 12 months)	2 Years (lag 13 to 24 months)	3 Years (lag 25 to 36 months)
In local currency									
Germany	0.77%	5.23%	0.077	−0.036	0.030	−0.027	0.019	−0.035	0.002
France	1.01	5.90	0.087	−0.050	0.068	−0.010	0.010	−0.020	0.028
Netherlands	0.93	4.80	0.098	−0.021	0.061	0.118	0.020	−0.019	0.005
United Kingdom	1.27	6.18	0.107	−0.111	0.102	0.028	−0.002	−0.021	−0.014
Switzerland	0.72	5.16	0.058	−0.091	−0.004	0.009	0.010	−0.021	−0.006
Japan	1.12	5.17	0.047	0.061	−0.026	0.002	0.013	−0.020	0.019
Canada	0.95	4.75	0.049	−0.060	0.025	−0.037	−0.006	−0.024	0.003
United States	0.92	4.36	0.021	−0.049	−0.004	0.028	−0.007	−0.028	0.012
In U.S. dollars									
Germany	1.07	5.93	0.029	−0.010	0.036	−0.054	0.017	−0.034	0.002
France	1.04	6.57	0.085	0.001	0.110	−0.053	0.021	−0.024	0.011
Netherlands	1.15	5.08	0.045	−0.044	0.082	0.057	0.016	−0.026	0.006
United Kingdom	1.20	6.85	0.087	−0.099	0.073	−0.010	−0.006	−0.009	−0.013
Switzerland	1.06	5.79	−0.012	−0.028	0.031	0.014	0.016	−0.025	−0.004
Japan	1.45	6.08	0.060	0.010	0.043	0.063	0.043	−0.027	0.008
Canada	0.92	5.09	0.027	−0.079	0.026	−0.072	−0.012	−0.025	−0.003
United States	0.92	4.36	0.021	−0.049	−0.004	0.028	−0.007	−0.028	0.012

TABLE 2. Currency Returns in U.S. Dollars: Sample Statistics, 1960–91

Country	Mean Return (per month)	Standard Deviation (per month)	Autocorrelation				Yearly Averages		
			1-Month Lag	2-Month Lag	3-Month Lag	12-Month Lag	1 Year (lag 1 to 12 months)	2 Years (lag 13 to 24 months)	3 Years (lag 25 to 36 months)
Germany	0.74%	2.89%	0.021	0.092	0.003	0.011	0.012	0.016	-0.026
France	0.75	2.75	0.010	0.104	0.053	0.000	0.013	0.019	-0.008
Netherlands	0.73	2.79	0.002	0.123	0.038	-0.025	0.018	0.014	-0.023
United Kingdom	0.73	2.71	0.080	0.078	0.014	-0.009	0.026	0.018	-0.011
Switzerland	0.71	3.30	-0.074	0.172	0.020	0.044	0.006	0.002	-0.021
Japan	0.85	2.72	0.052	0.033	0.064	0.085	0.028	-0.031	0.007
Canada	0.62	1.15	-0.010	-0.035	0.094	-0.064	0.050	0.055	0.011

TABLE 3. Bond Markets: Sample Statistics, 1971–91

			Autocorrelation				Yearly Averages		
Country	Mean Return (per month)	Standard Deviation (per month)	1-Month Lag	2-Month Lag	3-Month Lag	12-Month Lag	1 Year (lag 1 to 12 months)	2 Years (lag 13 to 24 months)	3 Years (lag 25 to 36 months)
In local currency									
Germany	0.65%	1.75%	0.163	0.044	0.025	0.005	0.047	-0.017	-0.013
France	0.89	2.03	0.171	-0.054	0.175	-0.021	0.053	0.011	-0.001
Netherlands	0.69	1.73	0.251	0.057	0.045	0.076	0.038	-0.031	-0.008
United Kingdom	0.94	3.27	-0.026	0.002	-0.297	0.024	-0.017	-0.004	-0.020
Switzerland	0.39	1.00	0.372	0.076	0.090	0.101	0.110	-0.020	-0.094
Japan	0.70	1.87	0.181	0.021	0.006	0.063	0.044	-0.024	-0.032
Canada	0.77	2.65	0.103	-0.053	0.046	0.075	0.024	-0.016	-0.001
United States	0.73	2.56	0.123	-0.109	-0.084	-0.022	0.021	-0.020	-0.003
In U.S. dollars									
Germany	1.08	4.26	0.026	0.056	-0.038	-0.044	0.011	0.010	-0.020
France	0.98	4.06	0.017	0.058	0.097	-0.026	0.034	0.006	-0.015
Netherlands	1.06	4.02	0.091	0.059	0.006	-0.037	0.013	-0.004	-0.031
United Kingdom	0.91	5.04	0.053	0.004	-0.194	-0.011	-0.010	-0.005	-0.009
Switzerland	0.94	4.21	-0.038	0.177	0.009	0.084	0.024	-0.005	-0.025
Japan	1.20	4.45	0.094	0.005	0.046	0.078	0.043	-0.036	-0.022
Canada	0.74	3.23	0.024	-0.071	0.012	0.032	0.007	-0.013	0.011
United States	0.73	2.56	0.123	-0.109	-0.084	-0.022	0.021	-0.020	-0.003

TABLE 4. Stock Markets: Sample Statistics, 1971–91

Country	Mean Return (per month)	Standard Deviation (per month)	Autocorrelation				Yearly Averages		
			1-Month Lag	2-Month Lag	3-Month Lag	12-Month Lag	1 Year (lag 1 to 12 months)	2 Years (lag 13 to 24 months)	3 Years (lag 25 to 36 months)
In local currency									
Germany	0.92%	5.26%	0.059	-0.060	0.115	-0.032	0.019	-0.036	0.010
France	1.28	6.40	0.079	-0.042	0.087	-0.050	0.007	-0.033	0.038
Netherlands	1.11	5.07	0.087	-0.023	0.027	0.139	0.008	-0.018	0.017
United Kingdom	1.50	7.00	0.099	-0.120	0.085	0.039	-0.016	-0.008	-0.018
Switzerland	0.67	4.96	0.089	-0.049	0.020	0.026	0.008	-0.024	0.008
Japan	1.25	5.34	-0.021	0.044	-0.054	0.043	0.018	-0.006	0.012
Canada	1.02	5.21	0.023	-0.029	0.064	-0.027	0.000	-0.028	0.001
United States	1.00	4.67	0.014	-0.047	0.001	0.054	-0.008	-0.032	0.020
In U.S. dollars									
Germany	1.32	6.27	-0.010	0.001	0.103	-0.079	0.020	-0.035	0.002
France	1.37	7.31	0.055	0.004	0.133	-0.100	0.024	-0.033	0.011
Netherlands	1.43	5.44	0.010	-0.042	0.055	0.044	0.004	-0.025	0.013
United Kingdom	1.46	7.85	0.081	-0.097	0.043	-0.008	-0.015	0.000	-0.017
Switzerland	1.18	5.95	-0.031	0.042	0.053	0.007	0.012	-0.029	0.007
Japan	1.75	6.62	0.007	-0.031	0.018	0.103	0.044	-0.013	0.001
Canada	0.99	5.67	0.002	-0.053	0.052	-0.066	-0.006	-0.030	-0.004
United States	1.00	4.67	0.014	-0.047	0.001	0.054	-0.008	-0.032	0.020

TABLE 5. Currency Returns in U.S. Dollars: Sample Statistics, 1971–91

Country	Mean Return (per month)	Standard Deviation (per month)	Autocorrelation				Yearly Averages		
			1-Month Lag	2-Month Lag	3-Month Lag	12-Month Lag	1 Year (lag 1 to 12 months)	2 Years (lag 13 to 24 months)	3 Years (lag 25 to 36 months)
Germany	0.92%	3.52%	-0.033	0.102	-0.030	0.007	0.017	0.001	-0.028
France	0.99	3.31	-0.041	0.131	0.036	-0.013	0.013	0.004	-0.020
Netherlands	0.93	3.41	-0.016	0.170	0.011	-0.040	0.021	0.002	-0.030
United Kingdom	0.93	3.23	0.072	0.077	-0.002	-0.017	0.024	0.008	-0.019
Switzerland	0.94	4.06	-0.096	0.196	0.004	0.042	0.006	-0.007	-0.027
Japan	1.04	3.34	0.039	0.015	0.062	0.078	0.027	-0.041	0.004
Canada	0.76	1.29	-0.050	-0.075	0.077	-0.090	0.029	0.028	-0.019

As seen in equation (3), the observed autocorrelation comes from the time variation in conditional expected returns. Conditional expectations adapt to changing economic conditions and tend to revert to long-term fundamentals. The best approach to make use of this phenomenon would thus be to model the time variation in expected returns directly as a function of a set of observable economic variables—as is done in the next section.

Modeling with the Information Variables

The risk premium on an asset is equal to its expected return minus the risk-free rate. Because this study is working with several nationalities, definitions of risk (and, therefore, of the risk-free rate) will vary according to the currency used. An asset's *national risk premium* is defined as its expected return in local currency minus its national risk-free rate. For example, the national risk premium on a French asset is equal to the expected return in French francs minus the franc short-term interest rate:

$$RP_{t+1}^{j} = E(R_{t+1}^{j}|\, \Phi_t) - r_t^{j}, \tag{4}$$

where RP_{t+1}^{j} is the risk premium on asset j estimated at time t for the next period, R_{t+1}^{j} is the local-currency return on asset j, and r_t^{j} is the local-currency interest rate. The realized excess return is defined as

$$X_{t+1}^{j} = R_{t+1}^{j} - r_t^{j}. \tag{5}$$

The *dollar risk premium* of an asset (that is, the risk premium on a foreign asset for a U.S. investor assuming no currency hedging) is its expected return in U.S. dollars minus the U.S. risk-free rate:

$$RP_{t+1}^{'j} = E(R_{t+1}^{'j}|\, \Phi_t) - r_t^{us}. \tag{6}$$

The realized dollar excess return is defined as

$$X_{t+1}^{'j} = R_{t+1}^{'j} - r_t^{us}. \tag{7}$$

Because of interest rate parity (the forward exchange rate premium is equal to the interest rate differential), the national risk premium of an asset is also equal to its dollar risk premium when the investment is fully hedged against currency risk. Indeed, the national risk premium is identical to the currency-hedged risk premium for investors from any country.[3]

The dollar risk premium of currency j is simply equal to the expected dollar return on an investment in the foreign short-term deposit (at the foreign interest rate) minus the U.S. interest rate. As a first approximation, the dollar risk premium on a foreign asset can be assumed equal to its national risk premium plus the dollar risk premium of its currency.[4]

A set of economic variables observable at time t, Z_t, is used to forecast period $t + 1$ returns. These economic variables are usually called *information variables*. The Φ_t information set reduces to a vector of n economic variables such that $Z_t = (Z_{1t}, Z_{2t}, \ldots, Z_{nt})$. The risk-premium model is assumed to be linear:

$$RP^j_{t+1} = E(X^j_{t+1}|\, Z_t) = b^j_0 + b^j_1 Z_{1t} + \ldots + b^j_n Z_{nt} = b^j Z_t. \tag{8}$$

Selection of Information Variables. Numerous studies have attempted to discover the information variables observable at the start of the holding period that help forecast returns of U.S. stocks over the period.[5] The economic information variables that have generally worked well for U.S. stock risk premiums are the dividend yield, the term structure spread (long-term minus short-term rates), the default spread (yield on risky or junk bonds minus yield on investment-grade bonds), the short-term interest rate level and its past change, and a seasonal term (January). These variables are clearly linked to the business cycle (see Fama and French 1989) and to changes in global uncertainty. The information-variable approach to modeling risk premiums has also been applied to foreign stock market indexes with positive results.[6]

---

[3] This is an approximation that assumes the full currency hedge is continuously rebalanced to adapt to movements in the asset price and, therefore, in the capital exposed to currency risk.

[4] This approximation holds exactly if no covariance exists between the asset and currency risks.

[5] See Ferson and Harvey (1991); Breen, Glosten, and Jagannathan (1989); Fama and French (1988a); Harvey (1989); Ferson (1989); and Campbell (1987).

[6] Bekaert and Hodrick (1992) examined the stock markets and exchange rates of Japan, the United Kingdom, and Germany for January 1981 to December 1989; Campbell and Hamao (1992), Japan for January 1970 to March 1990; Cumby (1990), Germany, the United Kingdom, and Japan for January 1975 to December 1987 using monthly observations of quarterly returns (hence, requiring an adjustment for overlapping); Cutler, Poterba, and Summers (1991), 12 foreign stock and bond markets and their associated exchange rates, with observations starting between January 1960 and July 1969, depending on the country, and ending in 1988; Harvey (1991), 17 foreign stock markets for January 1970 to May 1989; and Solnik (1993b), 8 stock markets and 8 bond markets for January 1971 to August 1990.

Models of the predictable time-varying component of currency returns that have been tested in the past generally indicate that the interest differential helps forecast exchange rate movements.[7] The currencies of countries with high interest rates (relative to other countries) tend to appreciate.

In light of previous studies, and given what international data are available, this study uses the following four national economic information variables: the short-term interest rate (r), the term spread (national long-term rate minus national short-term rate, LT), the dividend yield (DIV), and the short-term interest rate differential (national minus United States, DIF). National economic information variables are used for each national market. A January dummy accounts for seasonality, and the lagged return on the market accounts for short-term autocorrelation.

The following linear projections are estimated:

$$X_{t+1}^{j} = b_0^{j} + b_1^{j} r_t^{j} + b_2^{j} LT_t^{j} + b_3^{j} DIV_t^{j} + b_4^{j} DIF_t^{j} + b_5^{j} JAN_{t+1} + b_6^{j} X_t^{j} + \varepsilon_{t+1}^{j}, \quad (9)$$

where X_{t+1}^{j} is the monthly excess return over the one-month risk-free rate on an asset of country j (where the asset return and the risk-free rate are both measured in the national currency); r_t^{j}, LT_t^{j}, DIV_t^{j}, and DIF_t^{j} are, respectively, the one-month interest rate, the term spread, the dividend yield, and the interest rate differential of country j at the end of period t. JAN_t is a dummy variable that takes the value 1 if January is month t, and ε_{t+1}^{j} is a forecast error with, given the information variables, zero conditional mean.

Empirical Results. The national risk-premium model estimates for common stocks for the 1960–91 period are reported in Table 6. The coefficients' t-statistics are in parentheses, and the adjusted R^2s are also given. The national equity risk premiums are significant at the 10 percent level for all countries according to an F-test for each regression.[8] The average R^2 is approximately 5.5 percent. Although this adjusted R^2 looks low, the section titled "Tests of Dynamic Asset-Allocation Strategies" will show that it can lead to significant profit opportunities.

Some conclusions, valid for all markets, can be drawn from Table 6. The interest rate has a significant influence on the equity risk premium; the higher

---

[7] See Hodrick (1987) for a survey of the early work. See also Bekaert and Hodrick (1992), Cumby and Huizinga (1992), Cumby (1990), and Froot and Thaler (1990).

[8] The p-value (the confidence level at which the null hypothesis can be rejected) of the F-test is 0.06 for Germany and Japan and less than 0.05 for all other countries. The F-tests are not reported in order to keep the tables readable.

TABLE 6. National Risk-Premium Model Applied to Common Stocks, 1960–91

Country	b_0	b_1	b_2	b_3	b_4	b_5	b_6	R^2
Germany	-0.003 (-0.13)	-4.861 (-1.67)	-2.952 (-0.76)	10.913 (2.22)	2.049 (1.21)	0.009 (0.91)	0.119 (2.32)	0.029
France	-0.006 (-0.46)	-2.336 (-1.18)	0.177 (0.05)	5.288 (1.62)	3.057 (1.58)	0.030 (2.73)	0.078 (1.52)	0.039
Netherlands	-0.011 (-0.87)	-7.364 (-2.60)	-2.351 (-0.59)	12.099 (3.41)	0.493 (0.34)	0.034 (3.93)	0.089 (1.79)	0.095
United Kingdom	-0.051 (-3.17)	-2.660 (-1.65)	0.259 (0.08)	16.328 (4.29)	2.908 (1.81)	0.034 (3.10)	0.120 (2.39)	0.092
Switzerland	-0.014 (-0.85)	-7.368 (-2.06)	-3.752 (-0.81)	22.816 (2.85)	2.176 (1.85)	0.024 (2.46)	0.074 (1.45)	0.055
Japan	0.018 (1.28)	-3.737 (-1.70)	-0.915 (-0.25)	2.939 (0.95)	-0.539 (-0.46)	0.022 (2.22)	0.015 (0.28)	0.029
Canada	-0.027 (-1.69)	-2.629 (-2.19)	-0.392 (-0.14)	15.077 (3.02)	1.112 (0.61)	0.017 (1.94)	0.068 (1.31)	0.046
United States	-0.028 (-2.77)	-4.228 (-2.89)	2.035 (1.01)	17.113 (3.74)		0.015 (1.83)	0.018 (0.34)	0.068

The *t*-statistics appear in parentheses.

the interest rate, the lower the risk premium. The dividend yield has a large positive influence in all countries, which suggests that the risk premium is high in periods of high dividend yield (low stock prices). There is a positive January effect; this seasonal factor is statistically significant in all countries except Germany. Finally, some evidence exists of positive serial correlation in risk premiums; the coefficients are all positive, although in many cases, the significance level is low.

In addition to the poor quality of the interest rate data prior to 1971 for many countries, exchange rates were semifixed in the 1960s. Therefore, the study's detailed analysis and examination of the performance of dynamic strategies based on the risk-premium models is concentrated on the 1971–91 period. Table 7 reports results of applying the risk-premium model to common stocks (top panel) and bonds (bottom panel) for this period. The signs and magnitudes of the coefficients are similar to those reported in Table 6 for the 1960–91 period. The average adjusted R^2 is somewhat higher, however (7 percent instead of 5.5 percent), which suggests that expected returns on stocks have become somewhat more predictable than when the earlier years are included. The R^2s could also be confirmation of the better quality of interest rate data in the later period.

The expected returns for bonds are more predictable than those for stocks; the R^2 averages 10 percent. Most of the higher predictability comes from a strong positive autocorrelation in Swiss bond returns, however, which can be explained by the well-known illiquidity of the Swiss government bond market. Except for the autocorrelation term, the only variable that is significant (at the 5 percent level) for all markets is the term spread (the difference between the long- and short-term rates). This result suggests that expected bond returns are high when the term spread is large. In other words, investors should expect a drop in the long-term rate when the term spread is high.

The average R^2 for the currency risk-premium model (Table 8) is 8.3 percent. A few coefficients are statistically significant at the 5 percent level (for example, some weak evidence of a January effect is present), but the only strong systematic influence is the interest rate differential. The expected currency return is high when the interest rate differential (national minus foreign) is high. For example, the French franc tends to appreciate against the U.S. dollar when the French interest rate is high relative to the U.S. rate. (Remember that the dollar currency risk premium is equal to the expected currency movement for a U.S. investor [e.g., the French franc] plus the local interest rate [French interest rate] minus the U.S. interest rate.) The currency movement does not offset the interest differential, as many theories would suggest; it actually accentuates the differential. This finding confirms earlier

TABLE 7. National Risk-Premium Model Applied to Common Stocks and Bonds, 1971–91

Asset/Country	b_0	b_1	b_2	b_3	b_4	b_5	b_6	R^2
Stocks								
Germany	-0.002 (-0.06)	-5.135 (-1.55)	-2.068 (-0.48)	11.935 (1.90)	3.213 (1.47)	0.004 (0.36)	0.065 (1.00)	0.022
France	0.003 (0.13)	-3.212 (-1.13)	-0.532 (-0.13)	5.785 (1.42)	2.647 (1.22)	0.025 (1.66)	0.094 (1.46)	0.035
Netherlands	-0.006 (-0.31)	-7.704 (-2.10)	-2.620 (-0.53)	11.821 (2.94)	0.559 (0.34)	0.036 (3.10)	0.081 (1.30)	0.105
United Kingdom	0.021 (0.72)	-19.339 (-3.86)	-15.229 (-2.69)	36.534 (5.20)	3.650 (2.02)	0.047 (3.06)	0.145 (2.41)	0.158
Switzerland	0.009 (0.35)	-11.125 (-1.97)	-8.495 (-1.27)	22.012 (2.57)	3.224 (1.92)	0.022 (1.90)	0.054 (0.85)	0.060
Japan	0.046 (2.79)	-10.891 (-3.33)	-9.444 (-1.86)	19.743 (2.85)	0.666 (0.50)	0.018 (1.46)	-0.006 (-0.09)	0.067
Canada	-0.007 (-0.31)	-4.072 (-2.02)	-2.285 (-0.61)	13.232 (2.30)	1.216 (0.59)	0.016 (1.27)	0.019 (0.30)	0.042
United States	-0.021 (-1.45)	-4.653 (-2.04)	1.575 (0.60)	15.990 (2.99)	0.000	0.019 (1.79)	-0.012 (-0.19)	0.074
Bonds								
Germany	-0.015 (-1.96)	1.344 (1.24)	3.218 (2.34)	2.342 (1.15)	1.349 (1.87)	0.002 (0.58)	0.165 (2.68)	0.067
France	-0.012 (-1.95)	1.370 (1.57)	4.381 (3.47)	-1.172 (-0.95)	2.179 (3.23)	0.006 (1.22)	0.115 (1.82)	0.091
Netherlands	-0.019 (-2.77)	1.885 (1.50)	4.375 (2.65)	1.326 (0.96)	1.496 (2.70)	0.003 (0.76)	0.206 (3.21)	0.118
United Kingdom	-0.044 (-3.03)	6.202 (2.48)	8.791 (3.16)	-4.415 (-1.28)	1.517 (1.72)	0.012 (1.61)	0.013 (0.21)	0.062
Switzerland	-0.014 (-2.84)	1.014 (0.97)	2.943 (2.36)	4.328 (2.68)	0.284 (0.90)	0.000 (0.21)	0.285 (4.50)	0.250
Japan	-0.006 (-1.06)	2.090 (1.86)	5.706 (3.26)	-4.263 (-1.94)	0.848 (1.84)	-0.002 (-0.48)	0.176 (2.76)	0.084
Canada	-0.041 (-3.65)	1.999 (2.01)	6.338 (3.42)	6.973 (2.46)	1.087 (1.05)	-0.004 (-0.73)	0.086 (1.36)	0.080
United States	-0.011 (-1.46)	1.930 (1.53)	3.589 (2.46)	-0.868 (-0.29)	0.000	-0.007 (-1.15)	0.103 (1.59)	0.047

TABLE 8. Dollar Risk-Premium Model Applied to Currencies, 1971–91

Country	b_0	b_1	b_2	b_3	b_4	b_5	b_6	R^2
Germany	0.030 (1.82)	-0.727 (-0.33)	0.076 (0.03)	-5.082 (-1.23)	2.108 (1.45)	-0.017 (-2.12)	-0.006 (-0.09)	0.067
France	0.036 (3.44)	-3.143 (-2.14)	-3.559 (-1.69)	-2.033 (-0.98)	2.959 (2.65)	-0.012 (-1.61)	-0.062 (-0.95)	0.093
Netherlands	0.033 (2.31)	-3.492 (-1.36)	-4.054 (-1.19)	0.208 (0.08)	3.444 (3.00)	-0.014 (-1.78)	-0.057 (-0.86)	0.073
Switzerland	0.013 (0.88)	-1.941 (-0.79)	-3.415 (-1.24)	0.206 (0.06)	2.848 (3.19)	-0.004 (-0.60)	0.030 (0.47)	0.082
Japan	0.053 (2.55)	-7.840 (-1.73)	-9.249 (-1.72)	1.107 (0.16)	4.988 (3.61)	-0.025 (-2.67)	-0.102 (-1.61)	0.096
Canada	0.020 (1.94)	-1.837 (-0.88)	0.179 (0.06)	-0.408 (-0.09)	2.999 (3.49)	-0.012 (-1.60)	0.022 (0.34)	0.065
United States	0.013 (2.31)	-0.476 (-1.00)	-1.654 (-1.85)	-2.960 (-2.15)	2.157 (4.26)	-0.002 (-0.68)	-0.149 (-2.30)	0.108

studies (see footnote 7). The dollar risk premium of equity can be thought of as the sum of the national risk premium (given in Table 7) and the currency risk premium (given in Table 8), which is a good approximation because the covariance between stock market risk and currency risk is quite small.[9]

Data Mining and Snooping. This type of study runs an obvious risk, that of data mining—sifting through a large number of economic information variables until one (or some) with apparent predictive ability is found. Data mining would lead to spuriously high R^2s with little economic use; the relationship would be likely to vanish with a fresh data set (for example, a later period). This study avoided data mining by starting with a preestablished list of economic variables. All the variables, even those with little predictive power, were kept. If those variables had been discarded, the level of statistical significance (*t*-statistics) of the other variables would have improved.

The model used here is simple and similar for each country and market. In all cases, the same national economic variables are used. Quality of the data was assured, which restricted the time period, in order to avoid having the model's forecasting ability based on data errors.

Although not guilty of data mining, the study does risk the accusation of data snooping—that is, basically, using the data mining of other researchers. Previous studies showed that the model works well for the U.S. stock market. The risk of data snooping was reduced somewhat by this study's use of a more recent period than the period typically used to demonstrate the predictability of U.S. stock returns. This study also introduces a new data set of foreign asset returns and information variables. These data are correlated with U.S. data, however.[10]

Foster and Smith (1992) investigated data-snooping bias across correlated portfolios when using a small set of information variables selected from a large number of variables in order to maximize the regression R^2 of the original portfolio. They constructed a simulation in which they maximized the R^2 for the U.S. stock portfolio by selecting 5 information variables out of 50 candidates that were generated so as to be truly independent of the U.S. portfolio return. Then they fit the same 5 information variables across a number of foreign correlated portfolios in order to estimate the data-snooping bias. Their simulation indicated (see their Table 5) that a correlation of 0.4 across national

---

[9] For the sake of brevity, the results for the dollar risk-premium model applied to stocks and bonds are not reported; those results confirm this conclusion.

[10] Hedged foreign stock returns have an average correlation of 0.40 with U.S. stock returns over the period. The average correlation for bonds is approximately 0.33.

portfolios would induce an R^2 for the foreign forecasting regression of approximately 40 percent of the U.S. regression R^2. The data-snooping bias induced by the correlation implies, therefore, that the regression R^2 should drop by only 60 percent, not by 100 percent as suggested by the constructed independence between asset returns and information variables. The drop in R^2 should nevertheless be significant in the presence of data snooping.[11] In the present study, however, the reported results (see Tables 6 and 7) show, on average, no reduction in R^2 when moving from U.S. data to foreign data. This casual observation suggests that data-snooping bias is not strong in this study's international data.

Clearly, better performing models could be found, but even this simple model shows that the predictability of the time variation in expected returns is significant. Thus, the model can lead to high-performance global investment strategies, as will be seen in the section titled "Tests of Dynamic Asset-Allocation Strategies."

Modeling the Variance

So far in the study of the predictable components of time-varying expected returns, a stable variance of return has been assumed. This assumption is now relaxed in order to see if movements in the variance itself can be predicted. Clearly, markets go through tranquil and through agitated periods. The first question is whether these changes in volatility can be predicted to any extent in a systematic fashion. The second question is whether predicting these changes in variance can improve the prediction of asset returns—that is, can predict a change in conditional expected returns.

The most powerful methodology to model variations in conditional variance is the generalized autoregressive conditional heteroscedasticity (GARCH) approach. Heteroscedasticity simply means the variance is not constant over time. A good review of this approach can be found in Bollerslev, Chou, and Kroner (1992); Kritzman (1991) offers a lay introduction to the subject. The basic idea is that future variance can be modeled as a function of past variance and shocks or surprises in asset returns. In other words, the variance estimated in t for period $t + 1$ is conditional on the shocks observed at time t. Although the econometric methodology is fairly complex, the model is intu-

---

[11] Foster and Smith's empirical design is similar to that of this monograph's but with 250 observations instead of 251 and five information variables instead of four. The size of the total set of information variables in the current study before data snooping is not known, however (Foster and Smith used 50). In addition, the data-snooping risk of this study was reduced by using the foreign counterparts of U.S. information variables.

itive. A first-order, or GARCH(1,1), process can be written as

$$\sigma_{t+1}^2 = E\left(\varepsilon_{t+1}^2|\Phi_t\right) = \alpha + \beta\varepsilon_t^2 + \gamma\sigma_t^2, \tag{10}$$

where α, β, and γ are positive constants (estimated using a fairly sophisticated maximum-likelihood technique), and ε_t is the shock in the asset return equation (9). If a strong negative shock occurs in period t, the asset price falls and the asset return is well below its expected value, which leads to a large negative ε_t. The GARCH model tells us that the variance in the next period, σ_{t+1}^2 should be large because of the squared shock, ε_t^2. Large shocks, positive or negative, lead to an increase in the conditional variance. Remember that σ_{t+1}^2 is an estimate of the variance for period $t+1$ taken at time t and based only on information available at time t.

For the purpose of the present study, the major question is whether the modeled changes in variance enhance prediction of the asset returns. The search for the answer to this question leads to the so-called GARCH-M model, in which the conditional variance is assumed to influence the conditional expected return. In other words, the conditional variance, σ_t, is added as an explanatory variable in the risk-premium model of equation (9). Dropping the country superscript, j, for readability, the equation can then be written as

$$\begin{aligned} X_{t+1} = b_0 &+ b_1 r_t + b_2 LT_t + b_3 DIV_t + b_4 DIF_t + b_5 JAN_{t+1} \\ &+ b_6 X_t + \delta\sigma_{t+1}^2 + \varepsilon_{t+1}, \end{aligned} \tag{11}$$

where $\sigma_{t+1}^2 = \alpha + \beta e_t^2 + \gamma\sigma_t^2$.

Ordinary least squares cannot be used to estimate such a model; instead, one uses an algorithm that maximizes the log-likelihood function. The model estimates for common stocks over the 1960–71 period are reported in Table 9. (The b coefficients of the economic information variables are very similar to those in Table 6 and are not reproduced in Table 9 in order to keep the table readable.) The purpose here is to investigate whether the time variation in the variance of returns can be successfully modeled and whether this time variation has a significant influence on the conditional risk premium. A likelihood-ratio test is used to test these hypotheses.

The first step is to estimate the likelihood function for the constant-variance model of Table 6 (equation 9). This function is then compared with the likelihood function of the same model with a GARCH variance but no effect on the risk premium. Finally, the complete model of equation (11) is estimated with a GARCH model of the variance *and* an influence of the conditional variance on the conditional risk premium, as reported in Table 9. LR1 is the likelihood-ratio test that a significant GARCH modeling of the variance exists, and LR2 is the test that a significant influence on the risk premium exists. The LR test follows a chi-squared distribution.

The values of the coefficients α, β, and γ indicate the presence of a significant GARCH effect in the conditional variance. The β coefficients are positive for every country, and the t-statistics are significant at the 5 percent level. Table 9 shows a significant improvement in the likelihood function over equation (9), and all the LR1 tests are significant at the 5 percent level. The U.S. stock market has the weakest GARCH effect.

TABLE 9. Estimation of a GARCH-M Model for Common Stocks, 1960–91

Country	δ	α	β	γ	LR1	LR2
Germany	3.808	0.0010	0.111	0.868	28.6*	3.4
	(1.42)	(1.75)	(3.26)	(27.44)		
France	7.600	0.0010	0.094	0.757	10.4*	2.6
	(1.60)	(1.45)	(1.95)	(5.62)		
Netherlands	3.86	0.0006	0.040	0.959	28.2*	1.4
	(1.02)	(0.25)	(1.88)	(26.80)		
United Kingdom	4.334	0.0009	0.304	0.391	68.6*	5.2*
	(3.32)	(3.02)	(3.24)	(2.51)		
Switzerland	4.415	0.0010	0.067	0.913	10.8*	2.0
	(1.19)	(1.34)	(2.59)	(30.17)		
Japan	−1.920	0.0008	0.061	0.905	12.2*	0.2
	(−0.52)	(1.44)	(2.32)	(21.15)		
Canada	11.825	0.0002	0.048	0.944	15.8*	3.2
	(2.13)	(1.08)	(2.98)	(51.66)		
United States	7.411	0.0003	0.059	0.881	6.8*	1.4
	(1.20)	(1.33)	(1.92)	(14.60)		

* Significant at 5 percent level

Table 9 also indicates that the feedback of the conditional variance on the expected return is insignificant in most countries. The LR2 test (which indicates whether the addition of a conditional variance term in the mean equation is significant) finds significance at the 5 percent level for only one country (the United Kingdom) out of eight. To summarize, the GARCH effects are significant for all markets, but the influence of conditional variance on the conditional expected return (GARCH-M) is not.

Tests of Dynamic Asset-Allocation Strategies

So far, the analysis has established the *statistical* significance of the time variation in risk premiums in order to evaluate the predictive model's stability over time. Now, the analysis can turn to measuring and testing the *economic* significance of the time variation in risk premiums by looking at the performance of investment strategies based on the conditioning information set.

The investment strategy is mean–variance efficient at each point of time, based on the conditioning information set, and uses only public information available to investors at the time of selecting their asset allocations. The null hypothesis is that investors have no predictive abilities; hence, the conditional distribution reduces to the unconditional distribution. The test here uses a framework previously proposed by the author (Solnik 1993b) to test the out-of-sample performance of dynamic global strategies. The econometric procedure tests whether this dynamic strategy dominates the set of primitive assets and selected benchmarks in the sense of unconditional mean–variance efficiency.

Refresher on International Asset Pricing. The selection of a proper benchmark portfolio to measure performance is difficult even in a domestic framework, and the benchmark has a powerful impact on performance measurement, as stressed by Roll (1978). The difficulty is compounded by the fact that simple performance measures, such as Jensen's alpha, suffer from serious biases when applied to dynamic strategies with changing relative risks.[12] In an international context, the problems are even worse. Because of the presence of currency risk, international asset pricing models yield simple preference-free separation theorems only under very restrictive assumptions.

Solnik (1974), Sercu (1980), and Adler and Dumas (1983) showed that the pricing relationship of a traditional nominal capital asset pricing model (CAPM) applies to asset returns *hedged against currency risk* when the set of investment opportunities is constant (e.g., the set exhibits no stochastic inflation) and a nominal risk-free bill (comparable to a Treasury bill for the United States) exists in each currency. In this case, a pseudo separation theorem can be stated. All investors should hold a combination of their national risk-free bills and a common portfolio made up of the market portfolio of risky assets *plus* positions in all national bills. A forward currency position is then equivalent to going short in the foreign bill and long in the domestic bill; therefore, this common portfolio is often referred to as the world market

---

[12] For a review of these problems, see Grinblatt and Titman (1989).

portfolio hedged against currency risk. Note, however, that the word "hedged" does not imply a full hedge with unitary hedge ratios in each currency; it refers to a more complex, partial, multicurrency hedge. Only in the special case of currency risks and capital market risks being uncorrelated does the hedge become a simple unitary hedge ratio in each currency.

This common portfolio could theoretically be used as a benchmark, but its weights are not directly observable or easily estimated. In general, the weights of the national bills in this portfolio depend on parameters for individuals' relative wealth and risk aversion and, therefore, cannot be inferred from observable market data. The world market portfolio is part of this "common" mean–variance-efficient portfolio, but it cannot be used as the benchmark because, by itself, it is not efficient.[13] Without a theoretical benchmark, however, one cannot talk about the relative risk, or beta, of an asset. Therefore, although this chapter makes some comparisons between the performance of the dynamic strategy and that of the world market portfolio fully hedged against currency risk, the formal test does not assume a predetermined benchmark.

Design of the Dynamic Strategy. In the absence of an equilibrium asset pricing model, no assumptions are made about an optimal passive benchmark allocation or portfolios' relative risk measures. The dynamic global strategy will be a simple conditional mean–variance strategy. Informed investors will revise their beliefs about expected returns during the next period based on the previously discussed risk-premium models. They adapt their asset allocations accordingly. At the start of each month, an informed investor using the dynamic strategy reestimates the risk-premium model in the light of last month's data, forecasts excess returns using the current values of the conditioning information variables, and decides on an optimal conditional mean–variance asset allocation. A reasonable relative risk aversion of 2 is assumed.[14] There are no transaction costs, and short selling is not allowed. At the end of the month, the investor can observe the realized excess return; thus, a time series of asset-allocation weights and of realized returns is obtained.

---

[13] Similarly, IBM might be part of an efficient portfolio (e.g., the U.S. stock market index) but is not an efficient portfolio by itself.

[14] The relative risk aversion is equal to twice the investor's marginal rate of substitution of expected return for variance. A risk aversion of 2 is most commonly used in empirical work, but various levels of relative risk aversion from 1 to 10 have been simulated with similar qualitative results.

The conditional risk premium derived from the risk-premium model for asset j is denoted RP_{t+1}^j. It is a forecast formulated at time t of the excess return, X_{t+1}^j, for period $t + 1$. The investment rule can be written as follows:

$$\underset{w_t}{Max}\left[w_t RP_{t+1}^j - w_t'Vw_t \right]$$
$$w_{j,t} > 0 \qquad\qquad\qquad\qquad (12)$$
$$\sum_j w_{j,t} \le 1,$$

where V is the unconditional covariance matrix of excess returns, and w_t is the vector of portfolio weights, $w_{j,t}$, chosen at time t. Note that these weights do not necessarily sum to 1 because part of the asset allocation could be invested in the risk-free asset.

Note also that an explicit model for the conditional covariance matrix could be incorporated in the strategy design and that this strategy has presented evidence that GARCH models of the conditional variance differ from those of the unconditional variance. In this study, the focus is on conditional expected returns and a fixed covariance matrix is retained in order to separate the effects. Furthermore, conditional variances are much more stable than conditional expected returns, so the modeling of conditional covariances has less of an impact on the performance of the strategy than would the modeling of conditional expected return.[15] In any case, at present, the estimation of a 16-by-16 multivariate GARCH covariance matrix seems to be an impossible task.

Performance Testing.   With no a priori benchmark, this study cannot apply the traditional return/risk tests discussed in Grinblatt and Titman (1989) or in Gibbons, Ross, and Shanken (1989). The asset-allocation weights of the dynamic strategy can be observed, however, at each point of time; therefore, an approach proposed by Cornell (1979) and Copeland and Mayers (1982) can be applied.

The idea is that informed investors possess information on assets' conditional expected returns and build dynamic strategies that invest in assets with

---

[15] Cumby, Figlewski, and Hasbrouck (1991) studied optimal mean–variance strategies based on two countries (the United States and Japan). They did not model conditional mean returns, but they used various models of the conditional covariance. They conclude (p. 35), "While there clearly was time variation in variance and the E/G models did seem to capture some of it, the improvement in portfolio performance was somewhat limited."

high time-conditional expected returns. If their forecasting models have no value, the conditional distribution of asset returns reduces to the unconditional distribution. The null hypothesis is an independently and identically distributed unconditional distribution of asset excess returns, and an investor holding such beliefs about the return distributions is called "uninformed." To be able to conduct *t*-tests, the study also assumes joint normality of these distributions. For each time period, the return to be expected by an uninformed investor can be easily estimated from the asset-allocation weights observed at the start of the period. The performance test is, therefore, a direct comparison of the realized return on the dynamic strategy in each period, R^p, with its "uninformed" expected value, $E(R^p)$.

The details of the econometric methodology and tests can be found elsewhere (Solnik 1993b). The basic test relies on *t*-statistics comparing the realized return performance of the dynamic strategy with the unconditional expected value of returns. With the weights of the asset allocation at each point of time and the unconditional mean returns known, the return that could be expected on the dynamic strategy in the absence of any forecasting ability can be measured.

Empirical Results. Solnik (1993b) examined eight stock and bond markets from January 1971 to August 1990. Only currency-hedged returns were considered, and the risk-premium model used was somewhat simpler than the one developed in the section "Modeling with the Information Variables." The test had to be conducted out of sample by using a risk-premium model estimated for data anterior to the investment decision. The forecasts for period $t + 1$ were obtained as follows. The coefficients of the risk-premium model were estimated with the use of data up to period t. The information variables observed at time t were then used to formulate forecasts for the $t + 1$ period. Based on these forecasts, the optimal asset allocation at time t was then decided. In this procedure, the first years of data were omitted in order to obtain a significant estimation of the risk-premium models' coefficients, which reduced the testing period.

In the 1993(b) study, the author observed that the model's coefficients do not differ widely among countries. The coefficients of the risk-premium model for U.S. stocks and bonds over the 1960–70 period were estimated by using data from Ibbotson Associates. These U.S. coefficients were then used for all countries to make one-step-ahead forecasts for the first four years of the sample (that is, January 1971 to December 1974). The models for the stock and bond markets are, of course, different.

Starting in January 1975, the risk-premium models generate estimates for each country and asset type based on the domestic data from January 1971. The models' coefficients are reestimated each month to formulate one-step-ahead forecasts up to August 1990. This procedure allows use of the full sample.

Before looking at the results for the global strategies, take a moment to study the performance of purely domestic strategies. The top part of Table 10 reports the results of three types of dynamic domestic asset-allocation strategies. The first uses only the domestic risk-free asset and domestic stocks; the second uses bonds instead of stocks; and the third uses both bonds and stocks (a so-called three-way tactical asset allocation). The first three columns for each country report the excess returns of the domestic stock index, the domestic bond index, and an equally weighted mix. The relative weights of the bond and stock markets in the mix are set arbitrarily at 50 percent for each country to obtain a crude measure of the risk–return trade-off of a diversified bond-and-stock domestic portfolio.[16] The next columns report the realized monthly excess returns on the dynamic strategy, R^p, the uninformed expected return, $E(R^p)$, and a *t*-test of the mean difference between the realized and expected returns.

Consider first the domestic strategies. For all countries except Germany, the dynamic stock-only strategy produces greater returns and less volatility than the domestic stock index. The same comment applies to the bond-only strategy. In some countries, the mixed stock-and-bond domestic strategy yields performances that are more volatile than the benchmark, but the excess returns are much larger and so are the Sharpe ratios (excess return divided by standard deviation). For example, the U.S. mixed strategy yields a monthly return of 0.457 percent, compared with 0.038 percent for the benchmark with similar volatility. The average annualized difference is approximately 5 percent a year over 20 years.

The uninformed investor should be impressed by these numbers, but one should be cautious in their interpretation. The risk level of the dynamic strategy changes over time, and a conditional risk-pricing model is needed to avoid potential biases. The more direct *t*-test, however, which does not require a risk-pricing model, indicates, as reported in Table 10, that with the exception of Germany, the performance of all the strategies is superior to their uninformed expected values. In many cases, the unexpected return on the strategies is significantly positive at the 5 percent level.

Consider now the results of a global dynamic strategy as reported in the

---

[16] Although this percentage corresponds to an overall international breakdown of stocks and bonds in market capitalizations, the proportions vary somewhat among countries.

TABLE 10. Returns to Dynamic Domestic and Global Strategies, January 1971 to August 1990

Country	Benchmark Indexes			Dynamic Asset–Allocation Strategies								
				Stocks Only			Bonds Only			Stocks and Bonds		
	Stock	Bond	Mix	R^p	$E(R^p)$	t-Test	R^p	$E(R^p)$	t-Test	R^p	$E(R^p)$	t-Test
Domestic												
Germany	0.476 (5.16)	0.210 (1.78)	0.343 (2.94)	0.212 (3.65)	0.256	-0.18	0.114 (1.36)	0.098	0.17	0.158 (3.48)	0.277	-0.50
France	0.386 (6.44)	-0.060 (2.06)	0.163 (3.67)	0.435 (3.32)	0.096	1.65	0.038 (0.79)	-0.018	1.10	0.523 (3.27)	0.078	2.08
Netherlands	0.552 (5.16)	0.047 (3.34)	0.276 (3.41)	0.683 (3.30)	0.208	2.20	0.155 (2.20)	0.014	1.03	0.704 (3.24)	0.204	2.34
United Kingdom	0.523 (7.12)	-0.104 (3.33)	0.204 (4.47)	0.544 (4.79)	0.185	1.15	0.272 (2.29)	-0.029	2.01	0.738 (5.11)	0.185	1.60
Switzerland	0.277 (4.97)	-0.006 (1.06)	0.135 (2.71)	0.352 (2.56)	0.095	1.53	0.191 (0.63)	-0.003	4.72	0.338 (2.29)	0.075	1.75
Japan	0.790 (5.04)	0.092 (1.87)	0.441 (2.89)	0.835 (3.97)	0.452	1.48	0.282 (1.18)	0.042	3.12	0.992 (3.97)	0.447	2.10
Canada	0.222 (5.35)	-0.097 (2.67)	0.063 (3.29)	0.256 (3.00)	0.067	0.96	0.156 (1.43)	-0.330	2.90	0.390 (3.32)	0.043	1.60
United States	0.155 (4.70)	-0.078 (2.63)	0.038 (3.00)	0.545 (2.76)	0.050	2.79	-0.066 (1.39)	-0.034	1.10	0.457 (3.01)	0.018	2.23
Global	0.390 (3.90)	-0.033 (1.73)	0.201 (2.37)	1.348 (6.05)	0.509	2.09	0.294 (2.62)	0.012	1.64	1.322 (5.90)	0.441	2.20

Note: The first three columns give the mean monthly excess return over the domestic risk-free rate of the domestic stock, bond, and stock + bond indexes; standard deviations appear in parentheses. The next three columns give the excess return of the dynamic asset-allocation strategy (with the standard deviation in parentheses), its unconditional expected return, and the *t*-test on the mean difference between the two. All returns are expressed in percentages per month.

bottom part of Table 10. Here, the "benchmarks" are world indexes hedged against currency risk. The international indexes are weighted averages of the eight markets used in the study, where the weights are the market-capitalization weights at the start of each year. (Because relative weights are not available for the bond markets prior to 1981, 1981 relative weights are used for the prior years.) The benchmark statistics are provided for illustration purposes only, to describe a reasonable, well-diversified, passive international alternative to the global dynamic strategies.

The universe of the global strategy consists of the risk-free asset and 16 asset classes. Because the strategies are currency hedged, the excess return would be similar for any base currency, although the risk-free rate would be different. The stock-only global strategy allows investment in the risk-free asset and any or all of the eight national stock markets in such a way as to achieve monthly mean–variance optimization based on the forecasts of each risk-premium model.

The performance of the dynamic strategies exceeds that of the benchmarks and of the uninformed expected values. The realized excess return on the mixed strategy is three times larger than its expected value. The unexpected component is significant at the 5 percent level (*t*-test of 2.2) and averages to more than 10 percent a year. A similar conclusion applies to the global stock-only strategy. The realized return exceeds its uninformed expected value by 0.839 percent a month (approximately 10 percent a year) and is statistically significant at the 5 percent level (*t*-test of 2.09). The realized return on the bond-only strategy exceeds its uninformed expected value by 0.282 percent a month, but the *t*-test is only 1.64. Although this amount of superior performance is smaller than that for the global stock-only strategy, remember that the excess return on the global bond index was close to zero (slightly negative over the 20-year period).

Transaction costs would, of course, reduce the performance of these dynamic allocation strategies, but because futures markets exist for most of the asset classes, transaction costs could be kept to a minimum. With a conservative round-trip transaction cost of 0.1 percent on futures contracts, the performance of the mixed strategy is reduced only to 1.25 percent a month.

The standard deviations of the dynamic strategies are large and of the order of magnitude of the standard deviation of a single market. Clearly, the strategies are highly undiversified in each time period; often, an optimizing investor selects only one risky asset class (usually stocks). On the other hand, international indexes are well diversified, and their standard deviations are much smaller than those of their individual components. Note, however, that the Sharpe ratio—the realized excess return per unit of risk (standard deviation)—is at least twice as large for the dynamic strategies as it is for the corresponding benchmarks. A geographical breakdown of the global stock strategy shows that the portfolio tends to be fully invested in stocks most of the time. Europe (various markets) and Japan tend to dominate. The dynamic strategy was fully invested in European stocks in October 1987, resulting in a sizable loss. The overall good performance of the dynamic strategy is not explained by the exceptional performance in a couple of months resulting from the timing of market crashes in 1974 and 1987.

Another interesting comparison appears in the optimal asset allocation based on the unconditional moments.[17] As previously, the optimal asset allocation can be computed from the vector of expected excess returns and a relative risk aversion of 2. The unconditional expected return is estimated by the sample mean return; hence, the *ex post* performance of the asset allocation is equal to its unconditional expected return. For the global universe, the excess return on the unconditionally efficient asset allocation is 0.790 percent, with a standard deviation of 5.04 percent, compared with an excess return of 1.322 percent and a standard deviation of 5.90 percent for the dynamic strategy. The unconditionally efficient asset allocation, among the set of primitive asset allocations, with a standard deviation of 5.90 percent has an excess return of 0.861 percent, compared with 1.322 percent for the dynamic strategy using the conditioning information set. Again, the performance of the dynamic asset-allocation strategy is superior, although the comparison is somewhat biased in favor of the "unconditional" strategy: The dynamic strategy is based solely on *ex ante* information known prior to the asset allocation, while the "unconditional" strategy uses realized returns as inputs for expected returns in order to select the asset allocation. A similar conclusion can be reached for the stock-only and bond-only strategies. Clearly, dynamic strategies dominate the efficient frontier constructed from static portfolios of the primitively chosen assets. Moreover, the difference is economically large.

Currency Hedging

Currency hedging has become a hot topic in global asset allocation. The issue is more important in making allocations among bonds than among stocks, however, because currency risk is a larger component of the total risk of a foreign bond investment than of a foreign equity investment. Generally,

---

[17] The author thanks Bernard Dumas for suggesting this approach. Because of the obvious problems with statistical inference in this context, statistical tests for the performance comparisons are not provided here.

asset allocation and hedging are treated as a two-dimensional process: An investment manager decides market allocation and currency allocation separately. For example, a U.S. manager might decide to put 10 percent of a portfolio in Japanese yen bonds and 20 percent in Japanese equity but retain only a 15 percent currency exposure to the yen. In this case, half of the yen assets would be hedged against the yen/dollar currency risk.

Choosing a Global Benchmark and Hedging Policy. Currency hedging policy is an important component of the global benchmark set for asset allocation.[18] Typically, a fund manager will select a benchmark for the fund's long-term "neutral" investment strategy. The choice of a benchmark for global portfolios is a controversial issue, however. Domestically, U.S. pension plan sponsors have traditionally used separate benchmarks for separate asset classes rather than one common benchmark that includes all investable assets. For example, U.S. equities and U.S. bonds would have separate benchmarks. Investment managers extended this approach by creating a non-U.S. equity benchmark and a non-U.S. bond benchmark. For this purpose, most funds initially used as the stock benchmark a market-capitalization-weighted index of all non-U.S. stock markets, namely, the Morgan Stanley Capital International Europe/Australia/Far East (EAFE) Index.. Some investors prefer to use an index weighted to reflect countries' gross domestic product (GDP), which corrects the index according to the distribution of the productive economies internationally. For example, because most Japanese companies are publicly listed and trade at high price-to-earnings ratios compared with the rest of the world, the relative stock market capitalization of Japan is higher than its relative economic production. This difference is compounded by the large amount of cross-holdings of Japanese companies, which artificially inflates reported market capitalization. Some other investors believe that currency risks should not be borne and use a currency-hedged EAFE benchmark.

The choice of benchmark strongly influences investment strategy. Because of the relative independence of market movements from currency movements, international asset allocations that differ from the allocations of the benchmark can lead to marked differences in performance. The result is clear in the huge differences in performance, as reported by the major firms measuring international performance, of international money managers with similar mandates.

Given the importance of the benchmark and the debate about its choice, how should one choose? What are the desired attributes of a benchmark?

---

[18] Some comments in this section are drawn from Odier and Solnik (1993).

Based on the realities of international investing and performance measurement, a chosen international benchmark should have at least three properties: It should be widely accepted and easy to replicate, and it should have a strong conceptual foundation.

To assure that the validity and composition of the benchmark are not questioned, it should be accepted and used by other sponsors and managers. A benchmark that is not widely accepted by the profession is still useful, because it guides the international asset allocation of the money manager. Any benchmark also helps the client to structure a long-term strategy and sets a target for the money manager. Comparisons of a manager's performance with the performance of other managers operating under other, more widely accepted benchmarks will always be open to question, however, particularly if the maverick benchmark is easy to outperform.

A benchmark should require an asset allocation that can be easily reproduced in the marketplace as a long-term, low-cost, passive strategy. This criterion is not met when nonmarket weights are used. For example, tracking the performance of a GDP-weighted index with full currency hedging is extremely difficult and incurs heavy costs. Good tracking can require as high as 1 percent or more a year in transaction costs. Each time one national stock market goes up relative to the others, the manager must sell stocks to reweight the strategy to GDP figures, which are much more stable than market prices. Currency hedging is not viable in most currencies. Thus, using a GDP-weighted benchmark requires imperfect cross-hedging in the portfolio. It also requires constant and costly monitoring to rebalance the number of currency contracts to reflect cross-hedge ratios, stock market price movements, changes in the portfolio composition, rollovers, and so on. No investment strategy can exactly replicate the performance of a GDP-weighted benchmark.

Finally, the benchmark must have a conceptually strong foundation; it must rest on the belief that it represents the *efficient* passive alternative to an aggressive investment strategy. It is set as the objective to match or beat because it is regarded as the best strategy one could follow if the markets were fully efficient. The theory behind the CAPM has confirmed in the domestic milieu that the market portfolio (the stock index with market-capitalization weights) is the efficient portfolio that every single investor should be using as a benchmark if the market is efficient. The empirical evidence shows that beating the U.S. index is indeed quite difficult, even after risk adjustment.

Based on these three criteria, an important guide to determining the proper international benchmark is the answer to the following question: What does international asset pricing theory say is the optimal or efficient portfolio in a setting in which investors measure returns using different currencies?

What the Theory Teaches. International asset pricing theory has disturbing implications for hedging policy.[19] The theory concludes that all investors should combine their national risk-free bill with a common portfolio, often referred to as the world market portfolio *partly* hedged against currency risk. The problem is that the hedge ratios in currencies are different, and they depend on investors' preferences and relative wealth. For example, nationals of countries that are net foreign investors (such as Japan), or investors who have strong risk aversions have stronger needs to hedge foreign investment risks than do other investors. Therefore, the usefulness of the domestic CAPM, which claims that an *observable* market portfolio is efficient, disappears in the international setting; in contrast to market capitalizations, preferences and relative wealth are clearly not observable.

Recall what the theory does and does not say. It says that the world market portfolio (the "world index") should not be efficient; rather, it should only be part of an efficient portfolio. Similarly, the world market portfolio fully hedged against currency risk (i.e., with unitary hedge ratios) should not be efficient by itself. Therefore, although some universally efficient portfolio that could be used as a benchmark does exist, its weights are not observable.

Basically, therefore, an investment manager cannot know what the "neutral" currency-hedging policy is. The efficient currency-hedging policy consistent with market equilibrium is not known.

In the absence of a directing observable theory, all kinds of arbitrary a priori assumptions can be and have been made. Many managers and researchers have taken only a partial view of the theory, with results that are not consistent with international market equilibrium.

Some managers assume that currency risk carries no risk premium; hence, they suggest unitary hedge ratios to offset unrewarded currency risks.[20] This attitude basically attempts to minimize risk without considering expected currency return.[21] Actually, the risk-minimizing hedge ratio should be different from 1 if a correlation exists between the asset return and the currency movements (clearly the case for bonds, because exchange rates are correlated with interest rate movements). Unitary hedge ratios are apparently being adopted for the sake of simplicity.

---

[19] See Solnik (1993a), Adler and Solnik (1990), Adler and Dumas (1983), Sercu (1980), and Solnik (1974).

[20] See, for example, Perold and Schulman (1988).

[21] Furthermore, this approach attempts to minimize the risk of only the foreign part of the portfolio, not the global portfolio.

Another group of managers claims that currency risks cancel in the long run, and because currency-hedging policies are costly and time-consuming, they advocate a systematic no-hedging policy. This claim assumes that exchange rates exhibit reversion toward purchasing power parity. Indeed, the real exchange rate cannot diverge too much, or physical arbitrage will take place. Thus, the short-run volatility of the exchange rate should not be of extreme concern to a pension fund with long-term objectives. For example, the monthly standard deviation of the French franc/U.S. dollar exchange rate has been 3.31 percent a month since 1972, but the dollar moved only from 5.22 francs at the end of 1971 to 5.53 francs at the end of 1992—an annualized move of only 0.2 percent (5.9 percent over 21 years). The mean reversion is very slow, however, and to neglect currency risk completely, especially for bonds, seems to be foolhardy.

Other managers make arbitrary assumptions about the parameters of utility functions and relative wealth and derive various systematic hedging policies.[22] For example, a "universal hedge policy" with identical hedge ratios in each currency can be derived from such arbitrary assumptions as "identical risk aversion for all investors" or "no net foreign investment in any country." Even in the case of universal hedging, however, the amount of hedging is a function of the postulated world-market risk premium. Different sets of arbitrary simplifying (and unrealistic) assumptions yield different hedging strategies, but one has no way to tell which policy is "correct."

Another word of caution should be added. Theory tells us that the composition of each investor's equity portfolio should be equal to the world equity portfolio and that any hedging of currency risk should take place through forward contracts, not through the composition of the equity portfolio. For example, if the United States represents 40 percent of world market capitalization, the theory tells us that U.S. investors should hold 40 percent of their equity portfolios in U.S. equity and 60 percent in the EAFE Index. Assume, however, that a U.S. investor decides to hold 90 percent in U.S. equity and only 10 percent in foreign equity. The theory does not state that the 10 percent should remain invested in the EAFE. The optimal composition of foreign holdings is likely to be strongly affected by their relative importance in the total portfolio. Similarly, the optimal currency-hedging policy is likely to depend on the percentage of foreign assets in the total portfolio. Looking at risk alone, Jorion (1989, 1991) showed that the currency contribution is hardly

---

[22] See Solnik (1993a), Black and Littermann (1992), Adler and Solnik (1990), and Black (1989, 1990).

noticeable for portfolios with less than 10 percent invested in foreign currency assets.

Actually, taking some currency risk is a good diversification move against domestic budget, deficit, and/or monetary-policy risk, unless foreign assets represent a large proportion of the total portfolio.[23] Holding 5 percent of a portfolio in deutsche mark or other European Community currencies could, for example, provide interesting risk-diversification benefits for a U.S. investor, but the diversification advantage would disappear if European assets represented 40 or 50 percent of the total portfolio.

Finally, the optimal hedging policy will depend on the asset composition of the portfolio—especially whether the assets are foreign equity or foreign bonds.

To summarize, investment managers have no clear theoretical or pragmatic guides regarding optimal currency-hedging policies. They know the hedge ratio should not be 1 or zero, however; the currency hedge should only be partial. Moreover, they know it should differ among assets and vary over time.

The Empirical Importance of Currency Hedging. Changes in equity risk premiums are likely to affect the asset-allocation decision. Expected returns and asset risk premiums clearly change over time, and this study has provided evidence of a predictable component in the time variation of risk premiums on international assets. Everyone would agree that the risk premium on equity should stay relatively stable and should be positive because it is a compensation for risk in an asymmetrical market. The supply of equity is somewhat fixed, and investors bid prices up or down as a function of their expectations of profits and perception of risks. Most investors would agree that the equity risk premium should stay somewhere between 2 and 8 percent a year.

The bond situation is a contrast. The risk premium on a bond investment is equal to the expected return minus the short-term interest rate. Hence, the bond risk premium is linked to the relationship between long- and short-term rates. Loosely speaking, if investors prefer long-term investments while borrowers prefer short-term borrowing, a "negative risk premium" could exist. The reverse situation, however, is generally believed to hold.

The issue of a currency risk premium is even more delicate than the issue of a bond risk premium. For the French franc/U.S. dollar exchange rate to

---

[23] An increase in the budget deficit can lead to inflation, a rise in interest rates, and a drop in the value of the domestic currency.

have a positive risk premium, the U.S. dollar/franc exchange rate must have a negative risk premium. The equilibrium risk premium depends on the demand for currency hedging. This demand is affected by the net foreign investment position in each currency, the relative risk aversion of nationals of different countries, and economic conditions in the various countries. The sign and magnitude of the risk premium on each currency are likely to change over time. Thus, the optimal currency-hedging policy is going to vary considerably over time.

This conclusion can be illustrated by using the previous information variables and a similar empirical design (using only publicly available information to select the asset allocations). Consider three types of global dynamic strategies. The first strategy, which is similar to the strategies discussed previously, allows only fully hedged investments. The second strategy allows only unhedged strategies. In other words, one can invest across the world, but one cannot hedge the currency risk; the currency and market choices are thus necessarily linked. The third strategy allows separation of the market and currency decisions; partial currency hedging is allowed.

To facilitate the comparison, the analysis separates the universe of possible investments into equity-only and bond-only investments for the January 1971 to December 1991 period.[24] Table 11 reports the performance returns in excess of the risk-free rate of the three strategies compared with the performance of the U.S. market index. The strategies have the same volatility as the U.S. index; that is, the domestic and global performance is compared for the same risk level, in U.S. dollars.

For the period studied, the excess return on the U.S. stock index over the risk-free rate was 0.247 percent a month, with a monthly standard deviation of 4.67 percent a month. The out-of-sample performance of the global equity strategy with full currency hedging was much higher, at 0.694 percent a month for the same standard deviation. Because of the predictability of the currency risk premium, however, the performance of the unhedged strategy is superior to both, 0.962 percent a month. Allowing a separation of the market selection and currency selection provides a further improvement in performance—to 1.149 percent a month.

Results are similar for the global bond strategies. The excess return on the U.S. bond index was close to zero during these 20 years (–0.017 percent a month) with a standard deviation of 2.56 percent a month. Performance of the

---

[24] This empirical analysis differs from the author's previous study (Solnik, 1993b) as to the period covered. The earlier work studied the performance of strategies over the period January 1971 to August 1990.

TABLE 11. Performance in U.S. Dollars of Dynamic International Strategies with Different Currency-Hedging Policies, January 1971 to December 1991

		Mean Monthly Excess Returns			
Asset	Volatility (standard deviation)	U.S. Market	Full Hedge	No Hedge	Partial Hedge
Stocks	4.67	0.247%	0.694%	0.962%	1.149%
Bonds	2.56	−0.017	0.395	0.508	0.663

global bond strategies with the same standard deviation was 0.395 percent with full currency hedging, 0.508 percent with no currency hedging, and 0.663 percent with flexible currency hedging.

Conclusions

This study of the stock, bond, and cash markets of eight countries found significant evidence of predictable time variation in expected returns and risk across all markets. Mean reversion was found for all asset classes. The time to mean reversion depends on the asset but is fairly similar among countries. For equity markets in all countries, the mean reversion took between one and two years. For bonds, the mean reversion took between two and three years. Currency exhibited the longest time before mean reversion—at least three years. This finding confirms that "speculative bubbles" can exist for a prolonged time on the currency market.

Technical analysis could help an investment manager detect the trends and reversions. The conclusions here were based on simple autocorrelograms, but more sophisticated technical models could be of practical use. Investment managers should remember, however, that the performance of such models is very sensitive to the stability of the mean-reversion phenomenon. An increase or reduction in the length of time to mean reversion could make a technical model that was estimated with past data useless for the future.

A more productive approach than technical analysis would be to search for the underlying reasons for the observed phenomenon. Those reasons are likely to be linked to the business cycles in each country and in the international community.

Study of the influence of specific information variables on risk premiums (expected returns in excess of the risk-free rate) can enhance understanding of the predictability of asset returns. The study found that a predictable component in the time variation of asset risk premiums exists in most countries. The risk premium on equity is linked to the interest rate, the yield spread, the term spread, and the interest rate differential (local minus U.S. rate). This result is consistent with the business cycle having an influence on risk premiums, as explained by Fama and French (1989). Bond risk premiums were found to depend on the term spread, and currency risk premiums on the interest rate differential. This dependence is statistically significant and, perhaps more importantly, economically significant. Tactical asset allocation using these models of conditional risk premiums can, therefore, generate large profits.

The volatilities of asset returns vary over time in a somewhat predictable fashion. A GARCH model of the variance proved to be superior to an assumption of constant variance. Evidence is sparse, however, that this kind of time variation in volatility induces any change in the risk premium.

The final issue raised in this study was optimal currency-hedging policy. The theory suggests that the optimal global portfolio would be partly hedged against exchange risk; the theory is of little help, however, in determining the exact amount of currency hedging that should be implemented. A simulation over the 1971–91 period using the predictable risk premiums that were previously derived indicated that a strategy of selective hedging will greatly outperform a full-hedge or no-hedge strategy.

These findings have important implications for financial research and money management. Evidence is now ample that international assets' expected returns have a predictable component that can be identified by using some of the econometric methods outlined in this monograph. Although the risk always exists that the relationships found are suspect because of data mining or snooping, this study provides confirmation of previous findings (using a more recent time period and with a fresh set of data) and thus attests to the robustness of the phenomenon. More sophisticated models or additional information variables might increase predictability (but also the risk of data mining).

The performance of dynamic global strategies using these models proved to be quite good over the long run. The R^2s of the risk-premium models are quite low, however, so as many as 10 years will be needed to be reasonably sure that the dynamic strategies will outperform passive benchmarks. For many managers, 10 years or more might seem a very long horizon.

The findings of this study related to time variation in risk premiums can be interpreted theoretically in two ways. One interpretation is that the international financial markets are not yet fully efficient. A second interpretation is that the markets are efficient and the variation in expected returns is caused by a change in investors' risk perceptions and/or risk aversions.

If risk premiums do change over time, performance need not be measured by using unconditional returns and risk measures. As long as those measuring performance continue to look at sample mean returns and risk measures, however, an astute investor will appear to be achieving superior performance. Given the low correlation between stock and bond markets across the world, different asset allocations will yield markedly different performance.

Appendix.　Data Description

Common Stocks

Month-end stock market indexes calculated in local currency come from Morgan Stanley Capital International (MSCI), which since 1970 has also reported the stocks' dividend yields (calculated by averaging dividends paid over the preceding 12 months). For the period prior to 1970, dividend yields are those reported by the Organization for Economic Cooperation and Development (OECD). The MSCI sample covers approximately 60 percent of each market capitalization, and an attempt is made to stratify the sampling by industry breakdown so that each industry is represented in the national index in proportion to its national weight. The selection of individual companies is not, therefore, based solely on the companies' market capitalizations.

Bonds

Government bond indexes are from Lombard Odier and include price-only and cumulative bond indexes as well as average yields to maturity.[26] These bond indexes are based on a small sample of plain-vanilla, actively traded, long-term government bonds in each currency. Although the number of bonds in each index is limited, the bond prices and yields are current. These indexes have been published daily in the *Wall Street Journal* (Europe) since the early 1980s.

---

[25] Some researchers have used monthly foreign government bond indexes provided by Ibbotson Associates (Ibbotson, Carr, and Robinson [1982]), which were calculated prior to the mid-1980s by applying a simple duration model to average bond yields published by the OECD and the International Monetary Fund (IMF); a fixed duration was chosen for each country. Several methods to estimate bond yields are used by the reporting countries: In some, bond yields are the average yield of newly issued government bonds during the month; in other countries, they are the average yield to maturity on seasoned bonds with a fixed remaining life; in yet other countries, they are the yield to maturity on a selected benchmark bond (which changes over the years). Many countries have changed methods over time. The OECD and IMF tend to ignore the numerous optional clauses found in Europe, and the reported yields are calculated by using simple yield (Japan), semiannual actuarial yield (the United States), or annual actuarial yield (Europe).

Short-Term Interest Rates

One-month Eurocurrency interest rates represent risk-free rates. Eurocurrency rates are the only true market rates for many countries, and they are fully comparable, which is an important feature for the study.[26] All international researchers know how difficult it is to compare short-term rates across countries. Many countries have no "treasury" bill rates, and other short-term rates such as the call rate, discount rate, and rate on bond repurchase agreements (such as Gensaki in Japan) are often highly regulated and differ in tax treatment. As with bonds, an active market for many currencies developed only in the 1970s. The interest rate data come from Morgan Guaranty and Lombard Odier. National short-term interest rates are available for the 1960–71 period, and some summary statistics for the whole 1960–91 period are reported, but the comparability of data is questionable for the 1960s.

Exchange Rates

Month-end spot exchange rates come from the International Monetary Fund. Forward exchange rates are calculated by applying interest rate parity, and the relevant interest rate differential is "added" to the spot exchange rate.

---

[26] The volume of Eurodollar transactions is enormous, and the London Interbank Offered Rate has become the reference short-term dollar interest rate for borrowing in the United States. For example, the Eurodollar futures contract has the largest transaction volume in terms of underlying capital, and a similar comment applies to other currencies.

Bibliography

Adler, Michael, and B. Dumas. 1983. "International Portfolio Choices and Corporation Finance: A Synthesis." *Journal of Finance* (June):925–84.

Adler, Michael, and Bruno Solnik. 1990. "The Individuality of 'Universal' Hedging." *Financial Analysts Journal* (May/June):7–8.

Baillie, Richard T., and Ramon R. DeGennaro. 1990. "Stock Returns and Volatility." *Journal of Financial and Quantitative Analysis* (June):203–14.

Bekaert, G., and R.J. Hodrick. 1992. "Characterizing Predictable Components in Excess Returns on Equity and Foreign Exchange Markets." *Journal of Finance* (June):467–509.

Black, Fischer. 1990. "Equilibrium Exchange Rate Hedging." *Journal of Finance* (September):899–908.

———. 1989. "Universal Hedging: Optimizing Currency Risk and Reward in International Equity Portfolios." *Financial Analysts Journal* (July/August):16–22.

Black, Fischer, and Robert Littermann. 1992. "Global Portfolio Optimization." *Financial Analysts Journal* (October/November):28–43.

Bollerslev, Tim, Robert Y. Chou, and Ken F. Kroner. 1992. "ARCH Modelling in Finance: A Review of the Theory and Empirical Evidence." Working paper, Northwestern University.

Bollerslev, Tim, Robert F. Engle, and Jeffrey M. Wooldridge. 1988. "A Capital Asset Pricing Model with Time-Varying Covariances." *Journal of Political Economy* (February):116–31.

Bossaerts, Peter, and Richard C. Green. 1989. "A General Equilibrium Model of Changing Risk Premia: Theory and Tests." *Review of Financial Studies* (Winter):467–94.

Breen, W., L. Glosten, and R. Jagannathan. 1989. "Economic Significance of Predictable Variations in Stock Index Returns." *Journal of Finance* (December):1177–90.

Campbell, J.Y. 1987. "Stock Returns and the Term Structure." *Journal of Financial Economics* (June):373–99.

Campbell, J.Y., and Y. Hamao. 1992. "Predictable Stock Returns in the United States and Japan: A Study of Long-Term Capital Market Integration." *Journal of Finance* (March):43–70.

Cecchetti, S., and Pork-Sang Lam. 1990. "Mean Reversion in Equilibrium Asset Prices." *American Economic Review* (June):398–418.

Chan, K.C. 1988. "On the Contrarian Investment Strategy." *Journal of Business* (April):147–64.

Chang, Eric C., and Roger D. Huang. 1990. "Time-Varying Return and Risk in the Corporate Bond Market." *Journal of Financial and Quantitative Analysis* (September):323–40.

Conrad, Jennifer, and Gautam Kaul. 1989. "Mean Reversion in Short-Horizon Expected Returns." *Review of Financial Studies* (Summer):225–40.

Copeland, Thomas E., and David Mayers. 1982. "The Value Line Enigma (1965–1978): A Case Study of Performance Evaluation Issues." *Journal of Financial Economics* (November):289–322.

Cornell, Bradford. 1979. "Asymmetric Information and Portfolio Performance Evaluation." *Journal of Financial Economics* (December):381–90.

Cumby, Robert E. 1990. "Consumption Risk and International Equity Returns: Some Empirical Evidence." *Journal of International Money and Finance* (June):182–92.

Cumby, Robert E., Stephen Figlewski, and Joel Hasbrouck. 1991. "International Asset Allocation with Time Varying Risk: An Analysis and Implementation." Working paper, New York University.

Cumby, Robert E., and John Huizinga. 1992. "Testing the Autocorrelation Structure of Disturbances in OLS and Instrumental Variables Regressions." *Econometrica* (January):185–95.

———. 1991. "The Predictability of Real Exchange Rate Changes in the Short and Long Run." *Japan and the World Economy* (April):17–38.

Cutler, David M., James Poterba, and Lawrence H. Summers. 1991. "Speculative Dynamics." *Review of Economic Studies* (May):529–46.

Engle, Robert F. 1982. "Autoregressive Conditional Heteroskedasticity with Estimates of the Variance of United Kingdom Inflation." *Econometrica* (July):975–86.

Fama, Eugene F., and Kenneth R. French. 1989. "Business Conditions and Expected Returns on Stock and Bonds." *Journal of Financial Economics* (November):23–50.

———. 1988a. "Dividend Yields and Expected Stock Returns." *Journal of Financial Economics* (October):3–26.

———. 1988b. "Permanent and Temporary Components of Stock Prices." *Journal of Political Economy* (April):246–73.

Ferson, Wayne E. 1989. "Changes in Expected Security Returns, Risk, and the Level of Interest Rates." *Journal of Finance* (December):1191–218.

Ferson, Wayne E., and Campbell R. Harvey. 1991. "The Variation of Economic Risk Premium." *Journal of Political Economy* (April):385–415.

French, Kenneth R., G. William Schwert, and Robert F. Stambaugh. 1987. "Expected Returns and Volatility." *Journal of Financial Economics* (September):3–29.

Foster, Douglas F., and Tom Smith. 1992. "Assessing Goodness-of- Fit of Asset Pricing Models: The Distribution of the Maximal R^2." Working paper, University of Pennsylvania.

Froot, Kenneth A., and Richard H. Thaler. 1990. "Anomalies: Foreign Exchange." *Journal of Economic Perspectives* (Summer):172–92.

Gibbons, Michael R., Stephen A. Ross, and Jay Shanken. 1989. "A Test of the Efficiency of a Given Portfolio." *Econometrica* (September):1121–152.

Grinblatt, Mark, and Sheridan Titman. 1989. "Portfolio Performance and Evaluation: Old Issues and New Insights." *Review of Financial Studies* (Summer):393–422.

Hansen, Lars P., and Ravi Jagannathan. 1991. "Implications of Security Market Data for Models of Dynamic Economies." *Journal of Political Economy* (April):225–62.

Hansen, Lars P., and Scott F. Richard. 1987. "The Role of Conditioning Information in Deducing Testable Restrictions Implied by Dynamic Asset Pricing Models." *Econometrica* (May):587–613.

Harvey, Campbell R. 1991. "The World Price of Covariance Risk." *Journal of Finance* (March):111–58.

———. 1989. "Time-Varying Conditional Covariances in Tests of Asset Pricing Models." *Journal of Financial Economics* (October):289–318.

Hodrick, Robert J. 1987. *The Empirical Evidence on the Efficiency of the Forward and Futures Foreign Exchange Markets.* Chur, Switzerland: Harwood Academic Publisher.

Hodrick, Robert J., and Sanway Srivastava. 1987. "Foreign Currency Futures." *Journal of International Economics* (February):1–24.

Ibbotson, Roger G., Richard C. Carr, and Anthony W. Robinson. 1982. "International Equity and Bond Returns." *Financial Analysts Journal* (July/August):61–83.

Jorion, Philippe. 1991. "International Bonds: The Asset Class." In *Quantitative Global Investing*, eds. R. Aliber and B. Bruce. Homewood, Ill.: Dow-Jones.

———. 1989. "International Asset Allocation." *Investment Management Review* (January):41–49.

Kandel, Shumel, and Robert F. Stambaugh. 1988. "Modelling Expected Stock Returns for Long and Short Horizons." Working paper, University of Chicago.

Keim, Donald B., and Robert F. Stambaugh. 1986. "Predicting Returns in the Stock and Bond Markets." *Journal of Financial Economics* (December):357–90.

Kritzman, Mark. 1991. "About Estimating Volatility: Part 2." *Financial Analysts Journal* (September/October):10–11.

Lo, Andrew W., and A. Craig MacKinley. 1988. "Stock Market Prices Do Not Follow Random Walks: Evidence from a Single Specification Test." *Review of Financial Studies* (Spring):41–66.

Newey, Whitney K., and Kenneth D. West. 1987. "A Simple, Positive, Semi-Definite Heteroskedasticity and Autocorrelation Consistent Covariance Matrix." *Econometrica* (May):703–08.

Odier, Patrick, and Bruno Solnik. 1993. "Lessons for International Asset Allocation." *Financial Analysts Journal* (March/April):63-77.

Perold, André, and Evan Schulman. 1988. "The Free Lunch in Hedging: Implications for Investment Policy and Performance Standards." *Financial Analysts Journal* (May/June):45–50.

Poterba, James M., and Lawrence H. Summers. 1988. "Mean Reversion in Stock Prices: Evidence and Implications." *Journal of Financial Economics* (October):27–60.

Roll, Richard. 1978. "Ambiguity When Performance Is Measured by the Securities Line." *Journal of Finance* (September):1051–69.

Schwert, G. William. 1990. "Stock Volatility and the Crash of '87." *Review of Financial Studies* (Spring):77–102.

Schwert, G. William, and Paul Seguin. 1990. "Heteroskedasticity in Stock Returns." *Journal of Finance* (September):1237–57.

Sercu, Piet. 1980. "A Generalization of the International Asset Pricing Model." *Finance* (June):91–135.

Solnik, Bruno. 1993a. "Currency Hedging and Siegel's Paradox." *Review of International Economics* (June):180–87.

_____. 1993b. "The Performance of International Asset Allocation Strategies Using Conditioning Information." *Journal of Empirical Finance* (March):33–55.

_____. 1974. "An Equilibrium Model of the International Capital Market." *Journal of Economic Theory* (August):500–24.

White, H. 1980. "A Heteroskedasticity-Consistent Covariance Matrix Estimator and a Direct Test of Heteroskedasticity." *Econometrica* (May):817–38.

Selected AIMR Publications*

The Oil and Gas Industries, 1993 . . . . $20
    Thomas A. Petrie, CFA, *Editor*

Execution Techniques, True Trading Costs, and the
    Microstructure of Markets, 1993 . . . . $20
    Katrina F. Sherrerd, CFA, *Editor*

Investment Counsel for Private Clients, 1993 . . . . $20
    John W. Peavy III, CFA, *Editor*

Active Currency Management, 1993 . . . . $20
    Murali Ramaswami

The Retail Industry—General Merchandisers and Discounters,
    Specialty Merchandisers, Apparel Specialty, and
    Food/Drug Retailers, 1993 . . . . $20
    Charles A. Ingene, *Editor*

Equity Trading Costs, 1993 . . . . $20
    Hans R. Stoll

Options and Futures: A Tutorial, 1992 . . . . $20
    Roger G. Clarke

Improving the Investment Decision Process—Better Use of
    Economic Inputs in Securities Analysis and Portfolio
    Management, 1992 . . . . $20
    H. Kent Baker, CFA, *Editor*

Ethics, Fairness, Efficiency, and Financial Markets, 1992 . . . . . $20
    Hersh Shefrin and Meir Statman

Investing Worldwide, 1992, 1991, 1990 . . . . $20 each

The Financial Services Industry—Banks, Thrifts, Insurance
    Companies, and Securities Firms, 1992 . . . . $20
    Alfred C. Morley, CFA, *Editor*

Managing Asset/Liability Portfolios, 1992 . . . . $20
    Eliot P. Williams, CFA, *Editor*

Investing for the Long Term, 1992 . . . . $20

A New Method for Valuing Treasury Bond Futures
    Options, 1992 . . . . $20
    Ehud I. Ronn and Robert R. Bliss, Jr.

---

*A full catalog of publications is available from AIMR, P.O. Box 7947, Charlottesville, Va. 22906;
804/980-3647; fax 804/977-0350.

Order Form 023

Additional copies of *Predictable Time-Varying Components of International Asset Returns* (and other AIMR publications listed on page 44) are available for purchase. The price is **$20 each in U.S. dollars**. Simply complete this form and return it via mail or fax to:

AIMR
Publications Sales Department
P.O. Box 7947
Charlottesville, Va. 22906 U.S.A.
Telephone: 804/980-3647 • Fax: 804/977-0350

Name _____

Company _____

Address _____

_____Suite/Floor _____

City_____

State _____ ZIP _____Country _____

Daytime Telephone _____

Title of Publication	Price	Qty.	Total
_____	_____	_____	_____
_____	_____	_____	_____

Shipping/Handling
- ☐ All U.S. orders: Included in price of book
- ☐ Airmail, Canada and Mexico: $5 per book
- ☐ Surface mail, Canada and Mexico: $3 per book
- ☐ Airmail, all other countries: $8 per book
- ☐ Surface mail, all other countries: $6 per book

Discounts
- ☐ Students, professors, university libraries: 25%
- ☐ CFA candidates (ID #_____): 25%
- ☐ Retired members (ID #_____): 25%
- ☐ Volume orders (50+ books of same title): 40%

Discount $-_____

4.5% sales tax
(Virginia residents) $ _____

8.25% sales tax
(New York residents) $ _____

7% GST
(Canada residents,
#124134602) $ _____

Shipping/handling $ _____

Total cost of order $ _____

☐ Check or money order enclosed payable to **AIMR**   ☐ Bill me
Charge to: ☐ VISA   ☐ MASTERCARD   ☐ AMERICAN EXPRESS

Card Number:_____ ☐ Corporate ☐ Personal

Signature:_____ Expiration date: _____